Good Friday is a time of sadness,

Easter is a time of gladness.

On Good Friday Jesus died,

But rose again at Eastertide.

All thanks and praise to God.

This book belongs to

_____

_____

_____

Text by Lois Rock
Illustrations copyright © 1997 Illustrator Louise Rawlings
This edition copyright © 1997 Lion Publishing
The author asserts the moral right
to be identified as the author of this work
Published by
Lion Publishing plc
Sandy Lane West, Oxford, England
ISBN 0 7459 3733 0
Lion Publishing
4050 Lee Vance View, Colorado Springs, CO 80918, USA
ISBN 0 7459 3733 0
First edition 1997
10 9 8 7 6 5 4 3 2 1
A catalogue record for this book is available
from the British Library
Printed and bound in Singapore

NIGHTLIGHTS

Sad News, Glad News

LOIS ROCK

ILLUSTRATED BY LOUISE RAWLINGS

A LION BOOK

Long, long ago and far away
Was born a baby boy:
The baby Jesus. Angels said
He came to bring us joy.

what makes people
joyful?
Being well.

what makes people
joyful?
Being loved.

what makes people
joyful?
Feeling safe.

Jesus grew to be a man.
He was both good and kind:
He healed those who were ill and sad
And gave sight to the blind.

People were sad.
Jesus took away
their hurt.

People were sad.
Jesus wiped their
tears.

People were sad.
Jesus set them on
their way to
happiness.

He told of God, who made the world
And loves both great and small;
who clothes the flowers,
who feeds the birds,
who takes care of us all.

If God takes care
of flowers,
**God will take care
of us.**

If God takes care
of birds,
**God will take care
of us.**

If God takes care
of everyone,
**God will take care
of us.**

He said that God is overjoyed
When people turn from wrong.
And when they live
as God's friends should,
The angels join in song.

Why do the angels sing? Because there is less bad in the world.

Why do the angels sing? Because there is more love in the world.

Why do the angels sing? Because God has a new friend.

But some grew angry at these words:
'That man,' they said, 'must die.'
They whispered, plotted, lied—
and had him
Nailed to a cross so high.

Was Jesus really hurt?
Yes, sharp nails hurt his hands.

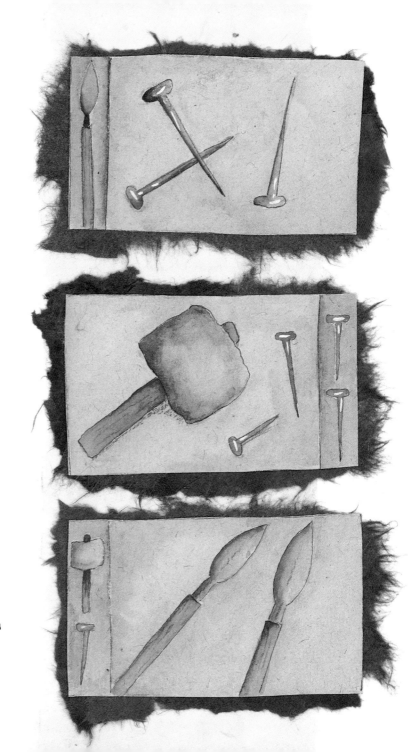

Was Jesus really hurt?
Yes, sharp nails hurt his feet.

Was Jesus really hurt?
Yes, a sharp spear hurt his side.

The sky grew dark: it might have seemed
That only bad would live.
But Jesus looked upon the world
And said to God, 'Forgive.'

what did Jesus forgive? He forgave all who do wrong.

what did Jesus forgive? He forgave all who do harm.

what did Jesus forgive? He forgave all the wrong that there is.

Then Jesus' friends, all weeping,
Laid his body in a tomb.
They rolled the stone door closed
And spent the next day deep in gloom.

Their friend
was gone.
So sad.

His love
was gone.
So sad.

Perhaps all
the good
things Jesus
had said
weren't true.
So sad.

Another day: the friends returned
To say a last goodbye.
But who had rolled the stone door back
Before dawn lit the sky?

who had moved
the stone?
**They didn't
know.**

Where was Jesus'
body?
They didn't know.

What should
they do next?
**They didn't
know.**

And then they saw them:
angels bright,
who said, 'You must not cry.
For Jesus is alive again—
God's love can never die.'

Really alive?
That's what the angels said.

Really alive?
Yes, they saw him!

Really alive?
Yes, they touched him!

So celebrate glad Easter news:
All bad things are forgiven.
God's gentle love fills all the world

Sing, because all
badness is beaten.
Alleluia.

Sing, because God's
love is so strong.
Alleluia.

Sing, because Jesus
has brought the
world joy.
Alleluia.

And Jesus Christ is risen.